12 Greek Poems after Cavafy

edited by
Paschalis Nikolaou

translated by
Paschalis Nikolaou
& Richard Berengarten

PASCHALIS NIKOLAOU has previously co-edited *Translating Selves: Experience and Identity between Languages and Literatures* (Continuum, 2008). He lives in Corfu, where he is Lecturer in Literary Translation at the Ionian University.

RICHARD BERENGARTEN is a poet who lives in Cambridge. His most recent Shearsman volume is *Notness: Metaphysical Sonnets* (2015). His co-translations from Greek include books by Antonis Samarakis and Nasos Vayenas.

First published in the United Kingdom in 2015 by
Shearsman Books Ltd
50 Westons Hill Drive
Emersons Green, BRISTOL BS16 7DF

Registered Office: 30–31 St. James Place, Mangotsfield, Bristol BS16 9JB
(this address not for correspondence)

www.shearsman.com

ISBN 978-1-84861-449-9

ACKNOWLEDGEMENTS
Cavafy's legacy, both in Greece and internationally, has greatly benefited
over the decades from the philological attentions of a large number of
scholars. Though some of them are already featured or mentioned in this
book in their other capacities – those of poet or translator – thanks are
especially due to Peter Mackridge, David Ricks and Josephine Balmer for
their watchful eyes and valuable critical comments. Further thanks are due
to Nina Todorović for the cover image from her 'Marginalization' series
(2010-2011; see: www.ninatodorovic.com); and to the translators whose
work features in the English arrangement of Ilias Margaris' 'Compiling
Verses from Cavafy' on p. 23 and their publishers. Yannis Ritsos' 'The Poet's
Space' first appeared in the April-May 2005 issue of *The London Magazine*,
then edited by Sebastian Barker.

The press' website hosts 'A Note on Translating *12 Greek Poems after Cavafy*'
along with detailed credits, at this URL:
http://www.shearsman.com/ws-shop/category/805-chapbooks/
product/5527-paschalis-nikolaou---12-greek-poems-after-cavafy

The website of the Cavafy Archive, currently under the auspices of the
Onassis Foundation, includes a wealth of material by and on the poet.
See: www.cavafy.com/www.cavafy.gr

Περιεχόμενα / Contents

For, and After, Cavafy

Across the following pages C. P. Cavafy (1863-1933) is *expressed again* by poets writing in the same language as his own. Spanning one hundred years – including in this frame the last twenty of the Alexandrian poet's life – these *12 Greek Poems after Cavafy* are also illustrations of an unmistakable voice as it is being shadowed. Together, they locate a kind of echo-chamber within Greek letters, which includes the attitudes forming within the culture along with the modulations in critical reception over the course of decades.

'World literature' has long admitted the poet's continuous presence. Perhaps nothing confirms it as decidedly as do those frequent appearances, in so many different languages, of poems *à la manière de,* 'in the manner of', Cavafy. This is a poet whose relatively slight output – the 'canon' of 154 poems surrounded by fragments and notes, including the 'unfinished', 'unpublished', 'repudiated' poems, plus the journal entries and brief opinion pieces – has been intensely examined. The attention also extends to the few translations the poet produced between 1884 and 1895, of parts of works by Shakespeare, Keats, Shelley, Tennyson, Baudelaire and Dante. In Greece as well as in other countries, all this material has now been variously edited, (digitally) archived, reprinted (including in the poet's handwriting), republished, paired with paintings and photographs, translated and retranslated. In English alone there have been over half a dozen book-length translations in the first decade of the 21st century. Such repeated viewings are usually – if not exclusively – reserved for the dramatists and poets of the classical past. Cavafy's perceptive conversations with that past, in which peripheral episodes and (pseudo)historical personages come alive in all the constancies and contradictions of human thought and desire, have certainly played a role in his popularity. In poems like 'A Prince from Western Libya' (1928) or 'Myres: Alexandria, 340 A. D.' (1929), the reader communes with an enduring consciousness, an antiquity truly inhabited yet all the while linking to current experience and mores: *we compare ourselves.* As chosen or designed by Cavafy, these well-appointed moments, phrases and emotions attain universal relevance. It is perhaps not surprising, then, that this reason for revisiting the poet is also the aspect of Cavafy's method that is most readily copied.

The apparent simplicity of Cavafy's construction is another common explanation for 'excessive results' when it comes to both translation and imitation. After all, this a poetry first understood in story-telling capacity: describing settings and events, and teeming with characters, and their actions and dialogue. These elements are accented even in renderings that strike a better balance between semantic content and the very many poetic and subtle rhythmic effects that Cavafy – unlike some of his translators – never disregards. And yet: the primary impact of most of his poems depends on a narrative drift transmitted nearly intact in other languages and far more clearly observed than Cavafy's meticulous fusions of 19th and early 20th century poetic forms, or his distinctive merging of the demotic and purist strands of the Greek language, which were still very much competing in his time. (Even so, these exactly constitute the unprecedented newness picked up and amplified by the early *Greek* imitations and parodies.)

Those core decisions Cavafy made in Alexandria at the turn of the previous century have travelled well across linguistic boundaries, allowing for degrees of engagement: an *œuvre* concentrated enough and sufficiently uniform in tone to be savoured by the experienced reader of poetry in a single volume, and in full; and no less so, in snippets, whether quoted by magazine articles or glimpsed among the electronic aphorisms relayed by the user of social media – who may never have even read a complete poem by Cavafy. And, as happens with only the greatest of achievements in art, here is a style recognizable enough across cultural space to enable further meaning-making: a *literary register* routinely inflecting the voice of poets, entirely suited for adaptation or recycling at the hands of a wide range of international artists.

When it comes to a bilingual presentation of poems written for and after Cavafy by his fellow poets in Greece, what perhaps matters first is the sheer scale of what has been left out. Two existing Greek anthologies, *Παρωδίες Καβαφικών Ποιημάτων* [Parodies of Cavafy's Poems] and *Ελληνικά Καβαφογενή Ποιήματα* [Greek Cavafy-inspired Poems], both edited by Dimitris Daskalopoulos, together hold no less than 358 such works; and exhaustive as the investigation in these volumes may be, they both stop at the start of the new century, covering the years 1917-1997 and 1909-2001 respectively. So English readers would be right in sensing that the twelve poems translated here represent certain peaks within a very long chronicle. The intervals between the years of publication listed on the contents page are indeed loud – and wildly populated. A narrative more philological in nature emerges through these selections, indicative as they are of wider dialogues between poetic voices, forms and movements. In this sense perhaps *12 Greek Poems after Cavafy* also exists as a *brief* Century of Greek Poetry.

Production of Cavafy-inspired poetry in the Hellenic world precedes the writing that occurs in other languages (experienced in all its breadth in another anthology, Συνομιλώντας με τον Καβάφη [Conversing with Cavafy] edited by Nasos Vayenas in 2000; containing more than 150 foreign poems translated into Greek). This is only natural, since, despite some preliminary encounters – most notably the publication of 'Ithaca' in T. S. Eliot's *Criterion* in July 1924, translated by George Valassopoulo – the first book-length edition of Cavafy's poetry by John Mavrogordato appeared in English in 1951, a full eighteen years after the poet's death. By then, Cavafy's work was commonly praised. However, given the initially mixed if not downright adverse reception of Cavafy's dramatic new style by Greek literary critics and journal editors, not to mention poets of the stature of Palamas, in the first two or three decades his fellow poets responded almost to a climate of denigration, and through numerous ventriloquisms. Most of these pieces have little more than topical value: their lines are often the verbal equivalents of newspaper cartoons (of which there were also several) – elongating features accurately enough to mock the man and views behind a style deemed to be pretentious or unpoetic. Meanwhile Cavafy's 'slight angle to the universe' becomes celebrated, his genius championed by E. M. Forster and others. Indeed the shift in Greek literary attitudes towards the poet was also brought about through the 'many returns' of his work from abroad, including those *gains* of translation. At a certain point, Greek and foreign-tongued Cavafy-inspired poems began to harmonise, as they eagerly extended and relocated the gaze and energies of the originals. It is now hard to imagine that there was a time when the recipient of irony was the poet himself.

Which of these many Greek-speaking works should themselves also exist – or bear repeating – in English? This question has been partly decided through a borrowed shape: that of *12 Poems for Cavafy*; the small book Yannis Ritsos produced half a century ago, in 1963. Beginning from a title exactly resonating the closeness of poetries 'for' and 'after', the current selection both parallels and offsets that earlier sequence, in which a literary voice – and a life – has already been absorbed, told through another.

Here, through one of his poems extracted from that sequence, Ritsos is joined by eleven others. The new collation stretches chronologically from 1916, from one of the earliest significant imitations by Timos Malanos, to 2015, with an as-yet-unpublished poem by Dimitris Kosmopoulos which coincides with its first translation into English. Between these two, and leaving aside the very early, more culturally bound parodies, which poets have long outgrown – a part of literary history acutely recalled, however, in the poem by Parthenis, alongside Cavafy's ambiguous relationship with his critics, and Malanos in particular – the other places are taken up by poems that are not only significant in themselves but also frequently in meaningful dialogue with one another. Their makers range from names familiar to foreign readers, like Ritsos or Seferis, to as yet unknown voices such as those of Voulis, Oikonomou and Margaris that now cross the border into English together with Cavafy's. But for no author included here are these merely occasional poems or chance encounters: the work of all twelve has maintained a long and diversely held dialogue with that of Cavafy, and in many cases continued in these poets' critical writings, as with Seferis and Vayenas.

Indeed the main intention, even in a small selection of Cavafy-inspired poetry, has to be a true record of the variety and experiment, the harmonies as well as discordances, that Cavafy's poetry *inspires*. In this sense, *12 Greek Poems after Cavafy* comprises titles where a well-known tone is trained on further scenes from history and myth or later events ('Alexander of Macedon', "Gorse", 'At Chandragupta's Palace, 305 B. C.', 'Three Horses, Olympic Prizewinners', '16 March 2015, 6 p. m.'); those near-rewritings, variations on themes and interior metatextual reflection ('From the Greek', 'The Grammarian's Melancholy'); the biographical after-images where the poet's own life provides the drama ('C. P. Cavafy', 'Cavafy Writes to Malanos', 'The Poet's Space', 'The Suitcase'); and even direct quotation as experiment ('Compiling Verses from Cavafy'). The observing reader will of course soon realise – not least via the notes on each individual title that come at the end of this selection – that some poems occupy more than one of the groupings briefly listed here. For these are poetic compositions where elective affinities and wakefulness to the nature of creativity, *empathy* and *borrowing* both entangle with and explain each other.

Whether these poets and poems channel or address Cavafy, their inclusion in this anthology answers to more than an attempt to convey a part of Greek literary history and expression. Their place is earned at the moment they can also exist as poetry in English. Imitative ways into and out of Cavafy are of course already a form of translation, overlapping with a most active, critical reading. *Actual* translation, translation into another language, needs to communicate, as well, this part of their poetry.

PN
Corfu, March 2015

Μάριος Μέμνων (Τίμος Μαλάνος)

Ο ΜΑΚΕΔΩΝ ΑΛΕΞΑΝΔΡΟΣ (1916)

Του κ. Κ. Π. Καβάφη

Αλέξανδρος ο Μακεδών αρρώστησε μια μέρα·
οι φίλοι του – οι αυλοκόλακες κι οι τέτοιοι –
γράμμα του στέλλουν και τον ειδοποιούν
πως ο ιατρός του Φίλιππος σκοπεύει
να τον δηλητηριάσει.

Ο Αλέξανδρος που ήξευρε το τι αυτά σημαίναν,
γιατί τα τέτοια σπάνια στους βασιλείς δεν είναι,
κι είχε στον φίλον του μεγάλη εμπιστοσύνην,
απάντηση δεν έδωσε σε κείνους που – δήθεν –
τον αγαπούσανε κι ήθελαν να τον σώσουν.

Όταν λοιπόν μετά ήλθε κοντά του ο Φίλιππος,
τον είδεν, ησύχως, να διαβάζει την *Ιλιάδα*.
Σιγά στον ώμο τον χτυπά προσφέροντας
στον βασιλέα το ιατρικό σε κύπελλον.
Τότε εκείνος μισογερτός – μισοχαμογελώντας –
το πήρεν εις το χέρι του, κι ενώ στα χείλη
αφόβως το πλησίαζεν
(σ' αυτές τες περιστάσεις, να πρέπει η τόση πίστις;)
στον Φίλιππον έδιδε το γράμμα να διαβάσει.

Marios Memnon (Timos Malanos)

ALEXANDER OF MACEDON

For Mr. C. P. Cavafy

One day, Alexander of Macedon fell ill and
those close to him – court attendants and the like –
sent him a letter to warn him
that his physician Philip intended
to poison him.

Since situations of this kind are hardly rare for kings
Alexander, being well aware of what was going on
and having complete trust in his friend,
sent no reply to those who – apparently –
loved him so dearly and wanted to save him.

Later, when Philip came to see the king
he found him sitting calmly reading the *Iliad*
and tapping him lightly on the shoulder
offered him the goblet of medicine.
Whereupon the king, half-leaning, half-smiling
took it in one hand and, utterly fearlessly,
brought it to his lips
(in circumstances like these, should one be quite so trusting?)
and with the other gave Philip the letter to read.

RB/PN

Γιώργος Σαραντάρης

Κ. Π. ΚΑΒΑΦΗΣ (1939)

Η πόλη όπου γεννήθηκες είναι η Κωνσταντινούπολη,
Πόλη του μέλλοντος,
Ενώ εσύ, πολύ προτού πεθάνεις,
Μέσα στο παρελθόν έπαιζες ζάρια.

Όχι, η ζωή σου δεν είταν ωραία
Με τα μυρωδικά
Με τα βιβλία
Με τις εξαίσιες εκείνες
Αλλά ψεύτικες οπτασίες.

Αγάπησες ποτέ σου μια Ρωξάνη;

Ο Αντώνιος της ποίησής σου η Αλεξάνδρεια.

Yorgos Sarandaris

C. P. CAVAFY

The city where you were born was Istanbul,
City of the future,
While you, long before you died,
Rolled dice into the past.

No, yours wasn't the good life
With your spices
Your books
Your indeed exquisite
But deceptive mirages.

Did you ever love a Roxanne?

The Antony of your poetry was Alexandria.

RB/PN

Άγγελος Παρθένης

ΚΑΒΑΦΗΣ ΠΡΟΣ ΜΑΛΑΝΟΝ (1960)

«Τίμο, αλήθεια, επλήθυναν τελευταίως πολύ
οι στιχουργοί που με μιμούνται στα γραψίματά των·
τι φοιτηταί, τι δημοσιογράφοι, τι δικανικοί,
τι διπλωματικοί υπάλληλοι και τι γυμνασιαρχαι,
τι άλλοι απίθανοι, τέλος πάντων, κύριοι,
που αρέσκονται στου Λόγου τις στρεψοδικίες.
Καλά, θα με ειπείς, παλαιά υπόθεσις αυτή:
θυμήσου τον αείμνηστον Μαγνήν και τη Σεγκοπούλου
– έστω κι αν το επέτρεπον τα κληρονομικά δικαιώματά της –
αλλά, επί τέλους, Αλεξανδρινοί εμιμούντο Αλεξανδρινόν
κι αυτό, βεβαίως, τιμά πιότερο τους ιδίους.
Όμως, αυτός ο συρφετός των Αθηνών,
και των επαρχιών, και των λοιπών παροικιών μας
– δε λέγω, κολακεύομαι πολύ·
μα τι φρονείς εσύ γι' αυτήν την εκλαΐκευση μου;
Μήπως και με υποβιβάζει η διάδοσίς της;
Μήπως και η Φήμη μου χάνει κομμάτι;
Μήπως και η Ποίησίς μου πρόφασις είναι μοναχά;
Φρόντισε, σε παρακαλώ, να εξακριβώσεις
και να με αναφέρεις σχετικά».

Angelos Parthenis

CAVAFY WRITES TO MALANOS

"Timos, they do seem to have been doing rather well lately,
these versifiers who imitate my style in their writings,
these undergraduates, newspaper columnists, magistrates,
diplomatic attachés, headmasters, and suchlike,
interesting characters all of them certainly, who enjoy
occupying themselves with the vagaries of the Word.
I suppose you could say this has been going on for quite a while now:
think, for example, of the late Magnis, or Sengopoulos's widow –
though in her case, admittedly she did have some rights to the estate.
Well, at least they were Alexandrians imitating an Alexandrian,
which is a credit to them when all is said and done.
But as for this crowd of hangers-on in Athens,
and the provinces too, and those in our far-flung communities –
I can hardly deny that it's a compliment, of course it is;
but what in your view does this appropriation of my work mean?
Could it be that all this derivative material dilutes it?
Could it dull my Reputation? And could it even be
that my entire *œuvre* is no more than a fad or pretext?
Would you mind looking into the overall situation
and reporting back to me on this matter?"

RB/PN

Γιάννης Ρίτσος

Ο ΧΩΡΟΣ ΤΟΥ ΠΟΙΗΤΗ (1963)

Το μαύρο, σκαλιστό γραφείο, τα δυό ασημένια κηροπήγια,
η κόκκινη πίπα του. Κάθεται, αόρατος σχεδόν, στην πολυθρόνα,
έχοντας πάντα το παράθυρο στη ράχη του. Πίσω από τα
    γυαλιά του,
πελώρια και περίσκεπτα, παρατηρεί τον συνομιλητή του,
στ' άπλετο φως, αυτός κρυμμένος μες στις λέξεις του,
μέσα στην ιστορία, σε πρόσωπα δικά του, απόμακρα, άτρωτα,
παγιδεύοντας την προσοχή των άλλων στις λεπτές ανταύγειες
ενός σαπφείρου που φορεί στο δάχτυλό του, κι όλος έτοιμος
γεύεται τις εκφράσεις τους, την ώρα που οι ανόητοι έφηβοι
υγραίνουν με τη γλώσσα τους θαυμαστικά τα χείλη τους. Κ'
    εκείνος
πανούργος, αδηφάγος, σαρκικός, ο μέγας αναμάρτητος,
ανάμεσα στο ναι και στο όχι, στην επιθυμία και τη μετάνοια,
σαν ζυγαριά στο χέρι του θεού ταλαντεύεται ολόκληρος,
ενώ το φως του παραθύρου πίσω απ' το κεφάλι του
τοποθετεί ένα στέφανο συγγνώμης και αγιοσύνης.
«Αν άφεση δεν είναι η ποίηση, – ψιθύρισε μόνος του –
τότε, από πουθενά μην περιμένουμε έλεος».

Yannis Ritsos

THE POET'S SPACE

The black carved desk, the two silver candlesticks,
his red pipe. He sits almost unseen in the armchair,
with his back always to the window. Behind his glasses,
immense and pensive, he observes his interlocutor,
in plenteous light, himself hidden within his words,
inside history, with his own people, who are distant, invulnerable,
while he traps others' attention in the delicate reflections
of a sapphire he wears on his finger and, thoroughly prepared,
        savours
their expressions, the moment when imprudent adolescents
moisten lips with tongue in admiration. And he,
cunning, insatiable, carnal, the great innocent,
wavering entire like a scale in the hand of god,
between the yes and the no, desire and regret,
while the light from the window behind him
rests on his head a wreath of exoneration and holiness.
"If poetry is not absolution," he whispers to himself,
"then we wait for mercy from nowhere."

PN

Γιάννης Βουλής

ΕΚ ΤΟΥ ΕΛΛΗΝΙΚΟΥ (1963)

Του Καλλιμάχου επίγραμμα   εις τα λατινικά
μεταφρασμένο απ' τον   Ρωμαίον υπατικό
Κόιντο Λουτάτιο Κάτλο.   Για την επιτυχίαν
οι ειδικοί ας κρίνουν.   Οι άλλοι σταματούμε
σε κάποιαν αλλαγή,   που δίνει το κλειδί
αυτής της ασχολίας,   μα ανοίγει την καρδιά
και του μεταφραστή.   Εκεί, που στο πρωτότυπο
βλέπομε «τιν' ες παίδων»   και «νέοι» γενικά,
εις τα λατινικά   διαβάζομε «Θεότιμο».
Τ' όνομα θα 'ναι κάποιου   Έλληνος πιθανόν
ίσως και Τυρρηνού   ωραίου της Ρώμης νέου,
που τους τραβούσαν τότε   οι τέχνες του θεάτρου.
Πάντως από απλήν   αγάπη της ποιήσεως
δεν έγινε η μετάφρασις.   Ένας του Κάτλου έρως
την έκφρασή του βρήκε   εις το κομψόν επίγραμμα.

Yannis Voulis

FROM THE GREEK

An epigram by Callimachus   translated
into Latin   by the Roman consul
Quintus Lutatius Catlus.   How successfully
we shall leave to the experts.   The rest of us might well pause
to ponder certain alterations   which provide the key
to this particular occupation   while also opening us
to the heart of the translator.   Where, in the original,
we see the phrase 'one of the boys'   and 'adolescents' in general
in the Latin version   we read 'Theotimus'
i.e. a person's name.   Probably a Greek
or perhaps someone from Tyros   a handsome young man in Rome
one of the many at that time   attracted by the arts of the theatre.
Anyhow it was not entirely   for the love of poetry
that this translation was made.   One of Catlus's flames
found his way   into this elegant epigram.

PN/RB

Γιώργος Σεφέρης

«ΕΠΙ ΑΣΠΑΛΑΘΩΝ...» (1971)

Ήταν ωραίο το Σούνιο τη μέρα εκείνη του Ευαγγελισμού
πάλι με την άνοιξη.
Λιγοστά πράσινα φύλλα γύρω στις σκουριασμένες πέτρες
το κόκκινο χώμα κι ασπάλαθοι
δείχνοντας έτοιμα τα μεγάλα τους βελόνια
και τους κίτρινους ανθούς.
Απόμακρα οι αρχαίες κολόνες, χορδές μιας άρπας αντηχούν
ακόμη...

Γαλήνη.
– Τι μπορεί να μου θύμισε τον Αρδιαίο εκείνον;
Μια λέξη στον Πλάτωνα θαρρώ, χαμένη στου μυαλού
      τ' αυλάκια·
τ' όνομα του κίτρινου θάμνου
δεν άλλαξε από εκείνους τους καιρούς.
Το βράδυ βρήκα την περικοπή:
«Τον έδεσαν χειροπόδαρα» μας λέει
«τον έριξαν χάμω και τον έγδαραν
τον έσυραν παράμερα τον καταξέσκισαν
απάνω στους αγκαθερούς ασπάλαθους
και πήγαν και τον πέταξαν στον Τάρταρο, κουρέλι».

Έτσι στον κάτω κόσμο πλέρωνε τα κρίματά του
Ο Παμφύλιος Αρδιαίος ο πανάθλιος Τύραννος.

                                    31 του Μάρτη 1971

George Seferis

'GORSE'

It was beautiful that day of the Annunciation at Sounion.
Spring again.
Patches of greenery among rust-coloured rocks
and the red earth, and the gorse-bushes,
their big needles at the ready, and their yellow flowers.
In the distance, ancient columns, harpstrings still resonating.

Utter calm.
– What then could have led me to think of Ardiaios?
A word in Plato perhaps, tucked in the mind's grooves
that named the yellow shrub,
unchanged since those times.
That evening, I found the passage:
"They bound him, hand and foot", it says,
"they flung him down and flayed him
and dragged him off, gashing his flesh on gorse-thorns,
then tossed him, ripped to shreds, down into Tartarus."

Paying for his crimes in the underworld,
so perished the vile tyrant Ardiaios of Pamphylia.

31 March 1971

RB/PN

Ζήσης Οικονόμου

ΣΤΟΥ CHANDRAGUPTA ΤΟ ΠΑΛΑΤΙ, 305 π. Χ. (1976)

Τραγουδιστές, χορευτές, καμαριέρες,
κρασί και σοφιστές απ' την Ελλάδα.
(κατά Μεγασθένην και Αρριανόν)

Στη Συρία ξεπέσαμε
εκείνη κολυμπούσε δίπλα στην τριήρη μας
κοίταζα εγώ τις πραμάτειες για τις Ινδίες.

Τώρα, εδώ στην Barygaza
δυο αρπαγμένα κορμιά
πεταμέν' ανάμεσα σ' εμπορευμάτων στοίβες
αναπολούν την αδειοσύνη μετά το συμβάν.

Ντόπια χαρούμενα πλήθη, μελαψά.

Μας πούλησαν στου Chandragupta το παλάτι
σοφιστής εγώ κι η Φιλομένη χορεύτρια.
Όμως τώρα
μ' ένα περίεργο μείγμα γλωσσών της κατάρρευσης
βρέθηκα ξανά στη νέα Barygaza μας
μα η ξένη τριήρης που άλλοτε μας άρπαξε
το θεσπέσιο εκείνο πρωί απ' την Αντιόχεια
όπου η Φιλομένη κολυμπούσε
κι εγώ κοίταζα τα μείγματα πραμάτειας και λαών
η τριήρης ναυάγησε τώρα στο μεσόδρομο
κι ούτε νησιά, ούτε στεριές, ούτε ρευστό
στοιχείο δεν μας πνίγει.

Μονάχα μια αιώρα τυραννεί
της ιστορίας το διάδρομο.

Zisis Oikonomou

AT CHANDRAGUPTA'S PALACE, 305 B.C.

Singers, dancers, chambermaids,
wines and sophists from Greece...
(according to Megasthenes and Arrian)

We both ended up on the Syrian shore.
She swam alongside the trireme
while I checked cargoes destined for the Indus.

Now, here in Barygaza,
we're two broken bodies
tossed among piles of merchandise, abandoned
to remembering emptiness – after all that has happened.

Local crowds, dark-skinned, cheerful.

They sold us on to the palace of Chandragupta,
me the sophist and Philomena the dancer.
But now
a weird mix of tongues spelling ruin
finds me again in this new Barygaza of ours –
though that foreign trireme that snatched us
from Antioch one beautiful morning
when Philomena was swimming
and I was watching people mingling with their wares –
that trireme has now sunk mid-route
and there are no islands, no shores, no seas
for us to drown in.

No more than a dangling hammock is left
to disturb the corridor of history.

PN/RB

Ηλίας Μάργαρης

ΣΥΝΘΕΣΗ ΚΑΒΑΦΙΚΩΝ ΣΤΙΧΩΝ (1992)

«Εις σε προστρέχω Τέχνη της Ποιήσεως...»
Γιατί τα σπάσαμε τ' αγάλματά των,
γιατί τους διώξαμεν απ' τους ναούς των,
διόλου δεν πέθαναν γι' αυτό οι θεοί.

Δεν αποθνήσκουν οι θεοί. Η πίστις αποθνήσκει
του αχαρίστου όχλου των θνητών.

Όσα ημείς επαραστήσαμεν ωραία και σωστά
θα τ' αποδείξουν οι εχθροί ανόητα και περιττά
τα ίδια ξαναλέγοντας αλλιώς (χωρίς μεγάλον κόπο).

Λυτρώθηκε το κράτος επί τέλους.
Ο μιαρότατος, ο αποτρόπαιος
Ιουλιανός δεν βασιλεύει πια.
Υπέρ του ευσεβεστάτου Ιοβιανού ευχηθώμεν.

Εντός των ταπεινών μας εστιών
ας ζήσωμεν ολιγαρκείς και ποταποί·
εκβάλωμεν τους πόθους εκ των καρδιών,
ας παύσει πάσα προς τον ουρανόν ροπή.

Τους ευτυχείς οι άνθρωποι τιμώσι.
Και τους υμνούσι ψευδοποιηταί.
Αι πύλαι, πλην, της Φύσεως είναι κλεισταί
εις όσους αδιάφοροι, σκληροί γελώσι,
γελώσι ξένοι εν πατρίδι δυστυχεί.

Αν ευτυχής ή δυστυχής είμαι δεν εξετάζω.
Πλην ένα πράγμα με χαράν στο νου μου πάντα βάζω –
που στην μεγάλη πρόσθεσι (την πρόσθεσι των που μισώ)
που έχει τόσους αριθμούς, δεν είμ' εγώ εκεί
απ' ταις πολλές μονάδες μια. Μες στ' ολικό ποσό
δεν αριθμήθηκα. Κι αυτή η χαρά μ' αρκεί.

Ilias Margaris

COMPILING VERSES FROM CAVAFY

"I appeal to you, Art of Poetry…"
Because we have broken up their images,
because we have expelled them from their fanes,
in no wise are they dead for that — the gods.

The gods do not die. The faith
            of the ungrateful mortal mob dies.

What we portrayed as beautiful and proper
the enemies will reveal to be foolish and useless,
repeating the same things differently (without much effort).

The empire is delivered at last.
The vile, the appalling Julian
reigns no longer.
For most pious Jovian let us give our prayers.

Within our humble hearths
let us live lowly and contented with little;
let us drive out the yearnings from our hearts,
let every bent heavenward cease.

Mankind lauds the happy.
And poets false extol them.
But Nature's gates are closed to those
who, heartless and indifferent, laugh,
laugh: strangers in a miserable land.

I will not enter into whether I am happy or otherwise.
Still, the thought remains, one that never ceases to delight me,
that in the overall addition (the addition, that is, of all those I detest)
which runs to such huge figures, I am not to be found
as merely one item among so many. In that total
I was never tallied. And for me, this is happiness enough.

Νάσος Βαγενάς

ΜΕΛΑΓΧΟΛΙΑ ΓΡΑΜΜΑΤΙΚΟΥ (2001)

Στον Μιχάλη Πιερή

«Καθώς ολοένα βουλιάζουμε στο γήρασμα
του σώματος, της μορφής μας κ.τ.λ.
ή στο βαθύ αναπότρεπτο της μοίρας μας
(σε ελπίδες και σε άλλα κατάλοιπα),

χρειαζόμαστε σωσίβια για να επιπλεύσουμε,
φουσκωμένες λέξεις που να μας κρατούν στα κύματα,
όπως τα σκοτεινά, τ' αβύθιστα ρήματα
της Πυθίας, που δεν μπορούσαν να τα διαψεύσουνε».

Σχόλιο Ευδόξου του γραμματικού μετά την ανάγνωση
στίχων του Ιάσονος Κλεάνδρου του Κομμαγηνού,
ελεγειακών, σχετικών με την άνωση
του ποιητικού λόγου (αλλά εν μέρει και του κοινού).

Nasos Vayenas

THE GRAMMARIAN'S MELANCHOLY

For Michalis Pieris

"Inexorably sinking as we deteriorate,
with the aging of face and body, and all besides,
and the deep inescapability of our fate
(in hopes, not to mention other flotsam on tides) –

what we need is buoys to stay above water,
words that inflate to keep us afloat in our coracle,
like those dark and unsinkable sayings uttered
through Pythia, mouth of the Delphic Oracle."

So comments Eudoxos the grammarian, stumbling upon
certain elegiac lines by Jason Kleander of Kommagini,
concerning the buoyant effects of poetic expression
(even though in the *koine* this buoyancy is also seen).

RB/PN

Διονύσης Καψάλης

Η ΒΑΛΙΤΣΑ (2003)

Γέμισαν μια μικρή δερμάτινη βαλίτσα
με κάτι ρούχα και χαρτιά που χρειαζόταν
τις λίγες μέρες που θα έμενε εκεί·
κι όταν την είδε, έτσι λέει μια μαρτυρία,
δεν άντεξε, τον έπιασαν τα κλάματα.

Την είχε πάρει ένα βράδυ βιαστικά
που πήγαινε στο Κάιρο να διασκεδάσει,
τριάντα χρόνια πριν, πάνε τριάντα χρόνια.

Αυτά τους έγραψε σ' ένα χαρτί. Κανείς τους
δεν ρώτησε τι έκανε στο Κάιρο,
για ποια διασκέδασή του πήρε τη βαλίτσα
κι έφυγε τόσο βιαστικά μέσα στη νύχτα·
κι ούτε κανείς τον ρώτησε τί τα 'θελε
τόσα χαρτιά μαζί του στο νοσοκομείο
αφού σε λίγες μέρες θα επέστρεφε
στο σπίτι του· μόνο κοιτάχτηκαν βουβά
όταν τους ένευσε να κλείσουν τη βαλίτσα.

Dionysis Kapsalis

THE SUITCASE

They packed a small leather suitcase for him
with some clothes and the papers he would need
for the few days he would be spending there
and when he saw it, so the story goes,
he couldn't bear it and began to cry.

He had bought it in a hurry one of those evenings
when he had gone off to Cairo for a change of scene
thirty years ago, it must have been at least thirty years.

That is what he wrote down on a piece of paper.
No-one had asked what he had been doing in Cairo,
or what kind of scene he had needed a suitcase for
when he had slipped off into the night in such a hurry.
Nor did anyone ask him why he needed
to take so many papers with him into hospital
since he would be up and back home again
in a few days. They merely looked at each other in silence
when he gestured to them to close the suitcase.

PN/RB

Κυριάκος Χαραλαμπίδης

ΤΡΕΙΣ ΙΠΠΟΙ ΟΛΥΜΠΙΟΝΙΚΕΣ (2013)

Σε τάφο στον Κεραμεικό χαμογελούν
τρεις ίπποι ολυμπιονίκες
γιομάτοι αυτοπεποίθηση· ανάγκη πλέον καμία
τα στυγερά ξωθιάς μαλλιά να περιπλέκουν
με την δική τους χαίτη και το χαλινό.

Ελένη δεν υπάρχει πια, το ξέρουν
από την φύση τους και το βιώνουν –
γι' αυτούς έχει τελειώσει ο στεναγμός.

Τρεις ολομέταξοι ολυμπιονίκες
ίπποι γιορτάζουν μ' ενθουσιασμό
τον ιδεαλισμό που κάποτε είχαν
και τώρα το πετσί του εν τάφω κείται.

Kyriakos Charalambides

THREE HORSES, OLYMPIC PRIZEWINNERS

In the cemetery at Kerameikos, three
horses, Olympic prizewinners, smile
brimming with confidence. They no
longer need to entangle manes or bridles
with the perilous long hair of the temptress.

Helen is no more, this they know. This is
borne out by their existence, their nature –
for them, now the heaving of sighs is over.

With such flare and sparkle, three
sleek Olympic-prizewinning horses
celebrate the idealism they once possessed,
whose hide has been laid to rest in the tomb.

RB/PN

Δημήτρης Κοσμόπουλος

16 ΜΑΡΤΙΟΥ 2015, 6 μ. μ. (2015)

Βαγγέλης Γιακουμάκης, εις μνήμην

Βρήκανε το κορμί σου σπαραγμένο από τ᾽ αγρίμια
σ᾽ απάτητο της λίμνης καλαμιώνα
κι η Μάρτυσσα η Μάνα σου συντρίμμια
μέσα σε πάγο φως διακαναλικού χειμώνα
ράγισε με το πρόσωπό της πέτρα
κι αδάκρυτη, στεγνή, μέρες τα χρόνια σου εμέτρα.
Βουβά στον θάλαμο του τηλεοπτικού νεκροτομείου
ψιθύριζε στην Παναγία: «Στου σφαγείου
ετούτου την αβάσταχτη την νέκρα
εισήλθε κι ο Υιός Σου, κι άμα θέλει
αρπάζει στην Ανάστασή Του τον Βαγγέλη».

Τά ᾽ξερες όλα τούτα πως θα γίνουν
κι όπως ταινία προσεχώς τα ζούσες
όταν τους άφηνες να δέρνουν και να φτύνουν
κι είσουν αρνάκι όταν η λύσσα τους μεθούσε.
«Είμαι περήφανη για το παιδί σου
γιατί σταυρώσαν την ψυχούλα του. Θυμήσου»,
απάντησε η Παναγία, απαλά.
Τά ᾽ξερες όλα τούτα. Τά ᾽ξερες καλά.

Dimitris Kosmopoulos

16 MARCH 2015, 6 p.m.

In memory of Vangelis Yakoumakis

They discovered your body ripped apart by wild beasts
by a remote lake, tangled in reeds and sedge
and your Martyr-Mother wrecked on grief's edge
in the wintry glare of programmed media feasts,
with her cracked face dry stone, without a trace of tears,
now she measures his years in terms of mere days.
Numbed in the chamber of the televised morgue
she prays to the All-Holy One beneath her breath,
"Into this slaughterhouse, through unbearable death
Your Son entered too. And if it be His will,
Vangelis also shall share in His Resurrection."

You know in advance all this will come to pass
and you live it out, like a film not yet released,
for when you allowed them to spit on you and beat you,
you were a lamb, as they were drunk on rage.
"Little mother, I am proud of your child,
because they crucified him, poor soul. So remember,"
the Virgin Mary gently replied to the woman.
You know this, all of it. You know it all too well.

RB/PN

Notes to the Poems, Poets and Translations

ALEXANDER OF MACEDON, p. 9. Timos Malanos (1897-1984) was one of the most influential literary critics in the early part of the 20th century to engage with Cavafy, whom he knew personally. He wrote the first book-length critical study, published in 1933, the year of the poet's death. Malanos' correspondence with George Seferis between 1935 and 1963 also touched frequently on Cavafy's work and the early debates among critics about the reception and evaluation of the Alexandrian poet.

'Alexander of Macedon' was published in December 1916 in the Alexandrian journal Προπύλαια [Propylaea] under the pseudonym Marios Memnon. It belongs to the first wave of Cavafy-inspired poems and is one of several imitations by Malanos.

C. P. CAVAFY, p. 11. The poet and essayist Yorgos Sarandaris (1908-1941) first published this short poem 'in the manner of Cavafy' as a privately circulated broadsheet in 1939. Apart from a number of such poems, Sarandaris was among the first to publish translations in Italian. These appeared in 1932 in the journal *Cronache*, Bergamo.

In 'C. P. Cavafy', a minimal psychobiography emerges from between known facts and felt intentions, only a few years after Cavafy's passing.

CAVAFY WRITES TO MALANOS, p. 13. Included in an early book of satires, this poem by Angelos Parthenis (b. 1935) imagines an episode that hinges on Cavafy's documented interest in the reception of his work. The poet's fictional letter here forms an ingenious comment on the dialogue between poets and literary critics. It suggests some ways in which the two capacities overlap, just as it takes stock of an accelerating situation in which literary enthusiasts have copied Cavafy's modes and styles. Parthenis' poem, though recognizing ironies, is of course part of the scene it describes.

Apart from his direct reference to Malanos in the title (see also pp. 8-9 above), two other names occur in this poem. Petros Magnis (1880-1953; real name K. G. Konstandinidis) was a contemporary of Cavafy's, who wrote several parodies and imitations. One of the libelous critical texts on Cavafy was attributed to him. Rika Sengopoulou (?–1956) was married to the inheritor of Cavafy's estate. After supporting the poet through his final illness, she and her husband co-edited the first publication of the 154 poems.

THE POET'S SPACE, p. 15. On the 30th anniversary of Cavafy's death, another of Greece's most significant modern poets, Yannis Ritsos (1909-1990) published a slim volume that remains an encompassing literary statement to this day. In *12 Ποιήματα για τον Καβάφη* (*12 Poems for Cavafy*, 1963), the poet is revealed in his surroundings in Alexandria, conversing with his circle of friends and readers, and during moments of composition. Taken together, Ritsos' twelve poems reflect an emerging myth of Cavafy as they trace the blurred borders between private and public space, lingering on items (the poet's glasses, his red pipe) which are both personal and literary. Ritsos' dramatised Cavafy is a lasting image of poetic voices in dialogue: thematic and stylistic inflections from Cavafy extend to other collections by Ritsos during the same period.

'The Poet's Space' opens Ritsos' empathetic sequence, which has been previously translated into English, notably by Rae Dalven and by Kimon Friar as well as, more recently, by Paul Merchant (*Twelve Poems about Cavafy*; Tavern Books, 2010). A translation by Karen Van Dyck is forthcoming from Red Dragonfly Press.

FROM THE GREEK, p. 17. Yannis Voulis (?-1975) wrote several poems influenced by an attentive and continuous reading of Cavafy. Relatively unknown even within Greek letters, as a translator he turned to the ancient poets from his native Samos, mostly to works included in the *Palatine Anthology* – on which Cavafy also drew for several of his historical poems.

Published in the same year as Ritsos' sequence, 'From the Greek' re-applies the long caesura space that effectively breaks a poetic line into two units. This form was regularly put to good effect by Cavafy in the latter half of his career (see e.g. 'Sophist Leaving Syria', 1926). Here, Voulis rewrites the 1925 poem 'Temethos, Antiochian, 400 A. D.', replacing the figure of the poet with that of a translator. The result conveys the energies felt in and flowing from translation as a literary act: it suggests how it is not just an original that can be 'for' or 'after'.

'GORSE', p. 19. Greece's first Nobel Prize-winning poet, George Seferis (1900-1971) often engaged with Cavafy, not least through his critical writings. Here, in Seferis' very last poem, the dialogue between the voices of the two poets is at its most poignant. Dated 31 March 1971, 'Ἐπί Ἀσπαλάθων…' is a reflection, in the middle of a seven-year dictatorship, on the inevitable fate of tyrannical regimes everywhere.

Several translations of this poem by Seferis have appeared, of which the most prominent are those by Edmund Keeley and Philip Sherrard in the *Complete Poems*, and Peter Levi's version, which is included in his memoir, *The Hill of Kronos* (1980). Levi's translation comes at the end of a vivid account of the visit by Seferis and several of his friends to Apollo's temple on Cape Sounion, Seferis' discussions with them, and his search for 'that word in Plato' (in *The Republic*, 616) which soon after, led to 'Gorse'. See also Seamus Heaney's retreading of the poem and its themes in his 2006 volume, *District and Circle* ('To George Seferis in the Underworld', p. 20-21), where a translation of one of Cavafy's 'hidden' poems can also be found.

AT CHANDRAGUPTA'S PALACE, 305 B.C., p. 21. Zisis Oikonomou (1911-2005) was born on Skiathos, where he also spent the final years of his life. His poetry is defined by an idiosyncratic application of modernist forms and a strong spiritual current that often encounters paradigms from Eastern philosophy. Combined with Oikonomou's lifelong interest in languages, it is not surprising that historical encounters between cultures are repeatedly dramatised, as in this particular poem, where his voice clearly draws on Cavafy's method. Following the death of Alexander, parts of northwestern India were reconquered by Chandragupta, founder of the Maryan dynasty. But swathes of territory remained under the sway of Hellenistic Kingdoms, and contacts were established through intermarriage between Greeks and Indians. Such arrangements also allowed individuals like the Greek historian Megasthenes, in his capacity as the ambassador of Seleucus I, to reside in the Maryan court. (The later historian Arrian mentions Megasthenes in *Anabasis Alexandri*.) In this region, during the last three centuries before Christ, languages and cultures frequently coexisted and overlapped, as did Hindu, Buddhist and ancient Greek religious practices. See also the 1920 Cavafy poem, 'Coins'.

Oikonomou received an award from the Athens Academy (1977) for the collection which included the poem printed here, as well as the Greek National Prize for Poetry (1995). A website dedicated to the poet features several of his works and critical perspectives: www.zisisoikonomou.gr

COMPILING VERSES FROM CAVAFY, p. 23. This medley of lines arranged by Ilias Margaris from several of Cavafy's poems was published in the literary journal *Periplus* (1992) and concludes with a complete short poem, 'Addition', written in 1897. Margaris' intention is both reflected and magnified here through already existing English versions. In 'Compiling Verses from Cavafy', the translations and translators that, in more ways than one, take the place of the original Greek, occur in the following sequence: (opening line) 'Melancholy of Jason, son of Kleander, Poet in Commagene, A. D. 595', 1921, tr. Evangelos Sachperoglou; (rest of 1st stanza) 'Ionic', 1911, tr. J. C. Cavafy; (2nd stanza) 'Memory', 1896, tr. Theoharis C. Theoharis; (3rd stanza) 'The Enemies', 1900, tr. Gregory Jusdanis; (4th stanza) 'A Great Procession of Priests and Laymen', 1926, tr. Edmund Keeley and Philip Sherrard; (5th stanza) 'The Tears of Phaeton's Sisters', 1897, tr. Rae Dalven; (6th stanza) 'Hours of Melancholy', 1895, tr. Daniel Mendelsohn. (Interestingly, 'Memory' is an early exploration of ideas later expressed in 'Ionic'.)

Thus the original bricolage has now been placed parallel to a new miscellany of the 'poet's other voices', as the latter have unfolded across time. This composite approach continues until the last stanza. There, the series of previous translational efforts culminates in a 2015 rendering of 'Addition'.

THE GRAMMARIAN'S MELANCHOLY, p. 25. An eminent critic and a leading poet of the 'Generation of the Seventies', Nasos Vayenas (b. 1945) has variously engaged with Cavafy across his work, not least in the essays of *Η Ειρωνική Γλώσσα* [The Language of Irony, 1995]. He was awarded the Greek National Prize for Poetry in 2005.

'The Grammarian's Melancholy' appeared in *Σκοτεινές Μπαλλάντες και Άλλα Ποιήματα* [Dark Ballades and Other Poems, 2001]. The lines reflected on by the grammarian are those written by Jason Kleander (or son of Kleander) from Cavafy's poem of 1921. A sonnet entitled 'Cavafy' from a later collection can be found in Vayenas' *The Perfect Order: Selected Poems 1974-2010* (London: Anvil Press Poetry, 2010), along with an English version of his essay on 'Cavafy's Poetry of Irony'.

THE SUITCASE, p. 27. Dionysis Kapsalis (b. 1952) has published over twenty collections of poems since the early 1980s, among them *Στον Τάφο του Καβάφη* [At Cavafy's Grave, 2003], on the 70th anniversary of the poet's death. This is an entire book inspired by Cavafy, in the mode of Ritsos. In this case however the poems were written at the request of composer Nikos Xydakis, becoming lyrics in the resulting 'musical portrait' entitled *Rue Lepsius*. The CD accompanied an edition of Cavafy's poems in 2013 – the next anniversary, in a stimulating instance of a dual presentation by the publisher Metaixmio.

Beyond his considerable output as an editor and reviewer, Kapsalis' translations include poems by Samuel Taylor Coleridge, Emily Dickinson, Matsuo Bashō, as well as several of Shakespeare's sonnets and plays, most recently *Hamlet* (2015).

THREE HORSES, OLYMPIC PRIZEWINNERS, p. 29. Kyriakos Charalambides was born in 1940 in a village which is now in the Turkish-occupied north of Cyprus; and his work, which often engages with the troubled modern history of the island, constantly negotiates strands of Greek language and literary tradition. Especially towards its end, this poem recalls Cavafy's 'The Souls of Old Men' (1901).

Charalambides is currently one of the most respected poets writing in Greek. He has received several significant awards, including the Cavafy Prize. A *Selected Poems*, with English translations by Greg Delanty, was published in 2005 (Cork: Southword Editions). In 2013 he was elected a Corresponding Member of the Athens Academy.

16 MARCH 2015, 6 p.m., p. 31. Dimitris Kosmopoulos (b. 1964) wrote '16 March 2015, 6 p.m.' following the discovery of the body of a young man, Vangelis Yakoumakis, in a suspected suicide. The title states, starkly, the date and time of this discovery. The 20-year-old had gone missing more than a month earlier, after being subjected to verbal and physical abuse from fellow students. Kosmopoulos has published eight collections of poetry and three books of essays since 2002. He received the Cavafy Prize in 2013, 150 years after the birth of the Alexandrian poet.

Kosmopoulos' poem converses with a poem of Cavafy's which records a deeply felt response to what later became known as the 'Denshaw Affair'. In 1906, in the Egyptian village of that name, violence erupted, leading to the death of a British soldier. In reprisal, the British occupiers publicly hanged five local males. Cavafy's title, '27 June 1906, 2 p.m.', presents the date and time of the execution of the youngest of the five. His poem expresses the lament of the boy's mother.

www.ingramcontent.com/pod-product-compliance
Lightning Source LLC
Chambersburg PA
CBHW021947040426
42448CB00008B/1273